Preserved Aircraft
of the World

US and Canada

GERRY MANNING

KEY
Books

Front cover image: With more than 100 airworthy examples in the USA alone, the North American Mustang is one of the most popular warbirds. P-51D Mustang NL751RB named *Glamorous Gal* arrives back at Farmingdale, New York, following a nearby beach-side air show performance.

Title page image: It may come as a surprise to some readers that all three of the aircraft in this picture, at Oshkosh, Wisconsin, are 'preserved' airframes. The McDonnell F-4D Phantom II and the two-seat Douglas TA-4J Skyhawk are operated by the Collings Foundation, while the single-seat A-4 is a privately owned example.

Back cover image: Based upon the Bristol Britannia but without the pressurisation, and piston engines in place of turboprops, the Canadair CL-28 Argus was a maritime patrol aircraft operated only by the Royal Canadian Air Force (RCAF). The prototype first flew in March 1957 and the type remained in service until 1981. CP-107 Argus 2 10742 is at Canada's Aviation and Space Museum, Ottawa, Ontario.

Published by Key Books
An imprint of Key Publishing Ltd
PO Box 100
Stamford
Lincs PE9 1XQ

www.keypublishing.com

The right of Gerry Manning to be identified as the author of this book has been asserted in accordance with the Copyright, Designs and Patents Act 1988 Sections 77 and 78.

Copyright © Gerry Manning, 2023

ISBN 978 1 80282 363 9

Typeset by SJmagic DESIGN SERVICES, India.

Introduction

The aim of this book, the first of three in this series, is to show a selection of the types of aircraft that are preserved around the world. Two more books will follow, one covering Europe and the third the rest of the world. There may be different views on what is meant by 'preserved'. For my purposes in these books, I have defined preserved as meaning aircraft occupying space in museums, those that are grounded, such as gate guardians, or an aircraft kept flying long after it would have have usually been retired. My selection includes many warbirds and vintage jets that can be seen at air shows.

Many museums choose to preserve military aircraft rather than civil ones, due to their interesting history and availability, but many of the flying vintage aircraft need to be recognised too. There is also a trend to preserve airliners, and this is most welcome.

I have included a wide selection of types, both old and new, and a broad selection of geographical locations. All the photographs are my own, taken on my travels.

Gerry Manning
Liverpool

America's first operational jet fighter was the Lockheed P-80. The prototype flew in 1944 and it later entered service with the US Army Air Force. It was redesignated F-80 in 1948 following the creation of the US Air Force as an independent service. F-80 Shooting Star 47-0215 is marked as '58612' at the Reflections of Freedom Historic Air Park at McConnell Air Force Base (AFB), Kansas.

The Republic Thunderjet, Thunderstreak and Thunderflash all had the designation F-84. The first of these, the Thunderjet, was designed as a replacement for the P-47 Thunderbolt. It was a straight-wing, single-seat fighter powered by a General Electric J35 turbojet. F-84C Thunderjet 47-1513 is also preserved at the Reflections of Freedom Historic Air Park.

The first of the swept-wing variants of the F-84 was the Thunderstreak. Its powerplant was a single Wright J65 Sapphire turbojet. Republic F-84F Thunderstreak 51-9480 is pictured at the Cradle of Aviation Museum, Garden City, New York.

The North American F-86 Sabre was one of the most widely used fighters of the 1950s and could be found, still in service, in the late 1990s in Bolivia. Many have been preserved around the world and some still fly for private owners. In 1948, Canada selected the type for its next fighter and decided to have it locally built by manufacturer Canadair. Canadair CL-13 Sabre 5 23257 is in the flamboyant markings of The Golden Hawks aerobatic team. It is preserved at the National Air Force Museum of Canada, Trenton, Ontario.

First flown in 1948, the Northrop F-89 Scorpion was a twin-engine, twin-seat, all-weather, radar-equipped fighter. More than 1,000 were built and its only operators were the squadrons of the USAF and Air National Guard. F-89J Scorpion 52-1949 is on display at the March Field Air Museum, California.

The North American F-100 Super Sabre first flew in 1953. It was the first fighter in operational service to achieve supersonic speed in level flight, as well as being the first of the so-called 'Century Series' of interceptors for the USAF. F-100C Super Sabre 54-1993 is at the Reflections of Freedom Historic Air Park, Kansas.

A long-range escort fighter, the second of the 'Century Series' was the McDonnell F-101 Voodoo. Its original task was to escort bombers of the USAF's Strategic Air Command (SAC) and later it operated for Tactical Air Command (TAC). As well as service with the Americans, it also operated for the air forces of Taiwan and Canada. CF-101B Voodoo 101038 is in the special markings of 416 Squadron, Royal Canadian Air Force, at the Reynolds Alberta Museum, Wetaskiwin.

A single-seat, all-weather fighter, the Convair F-102 Delta Dagger first took to the air in 1953 and entered service with the USAF two years later. F-102A Delta Dagger 56-1114 is at the March Field Museum, California.

Dubbed 'the missile with a man in it', the Lockheed F-104 Starfighter first flew in 1954 and passed the speed of Mach 2 the following year. The type saw service with many air forces around the world and was licence-built in Europe and Japan. F-104N Starfighter N812NA was used by The National Aeronautics and Space Administration (NASA) for test and trials' work. It is on display at the gate of the Lockheed/Martin Skunk works at Palmdale, California.

One of the most elegant air-defence fighters, the Convair F-106 Delta Dart incorporated a complete weapons system and was an extensive development of the earlier F-102. It remained in service with the USAF, the only air arm to operate it, until 1988. F-106A Delta Dart 58-0793 is marked as '0-72456' and can be found at the Castle Air Museum, Atwater, California.

A supersonic tactical fighter-bomber, the Republic F-105 Thunderchief first flew in 1955. It could carry conventional and nuclear weapons. As a bomber, it bore the brunt of air operations over North Vietnam and 397 aircraft were lost during the conflict. F-105D Thunderchief 61-0056 is on display at the gate of Seymour Johnson AFB, Goldsboro, North Carolina.

Still in front-line service with the USA and other air arms, the McDonnell Douglas F-15 Eagle first took to the air in 1972. F-15B Eagle 77-0161 is at the gate of Seymour Johnson AFB.

Launched in 1966, the Attack Experimental (AX) programme called for a rugged ground-attack aircraft. Two companies were funded to build prototypes to compete for the contract. The winner was the Fairchild A-10 Thunderbolt II. As well as the hard points under the wings for bombs and rockets, it has a 30mm GAU-8 seven-barrel rotary cannon. Still in service with the USAF, it has proved its worth in combat in several conflicts. A-10A Thunderbolt II 81-0987 is one of a number of aircraft at the gate of Seymour Johnson AFB.

In the AX programme, there were two designs in competition for the production contract, the A-10 won, and the Northrop A-9A lost. Both of its prototypes have been preserved. A-9A 71-1368 is at the March Field Air Museum, California.

Grumman's F-14 Tomcat was the last in a long line of Grumman 'Cats' for the US Navy. It was a two-seat, fleet defence fighter and found fame as the aircraft star of the film *Top Gun*. Out of service now with the US Navy, it can still be found flying in Iran. On display at one of the gates of Oceana Naval Air Station (NAS), Virginia, is F-14D Tomcat 164604.

A subsonic two-seat, side-by-side, carrier-borne, all-weather attack-bomber, the Grumman A-6 Intruder served with both the US Navy and the US Marine Corps. On display inside Cherry Point Marine Corps Air Station (MCAS), North Carolina, is YA-6A Intruder 147865.

A four-seat electronic warfare aircraft for carrier operations, the Grumman EA-6B Prowler was developed from the A-6 Intruder. It was operated by both the US Navy and USMC but has now been withdrawn from service. Pictured on a wet day at the American Air Power Museum, Farmingdale, New York, is EA-6B Prowler 162938.

One of the most versatile warplanes ever built, with a production run of more than 5,000, the McDonnell F-4 Phantom II was designed for use as an all-weather fleet defence fighter for the US Navy. So good was it that the USAF evaluated and adopted it into service. It can still be found in service with a number of air forces around the world. RF-4B Phantom II 157342, the photographic reconnaissance version, is at the Havelock Tourist & Event Centre, North Carolina.

The US Navy operates the General Dynamics (now Lockheed) F-16 Fighting Falcon for aggressor training at its Fighter Weapons School. The naval version is stripped down, without weapons, but has some extra structural strength due to the high g-forces placed upon it during its missions. F-16N 163576 is at the Air Power Heritage Park, Fallon Naval Air Station (NAS), Nevada.

Another type used by the US Navy for aggressor training is the Northrop F-5 Freedom Fighter. The design was produced as a lightweight fighter to be sold to allies of the USA and it was in production for many years. Later variants were named Tiger. More than 20 nations have or still operate them. F-5E Tiger II 160796 is at the Air Power Heritage Park, Fallon NAS.

During the early 1970s, the USAF granted funding for two companies to build prototypes of aircraft that met the specifications for a new lightweight fighter. The General Dynamics YF-16 and the Northrop YF-17 were built to compete in a fly-off against each other. The winner was the YF-16. The YF-17 was developed by McDonnell Douglas into the F/A-18 for the US Navy. F/A-18A Hornet 161708 is at the Air Power Heritage Park, Fallon NAS. Since Northrop had no experience in building naval aircraft, the company agreed that if it won the contract then Northrop would be the lead company, and if it did not then McDonnell Douglas would lead to bid for a navy contract.

Known as 'the last of the gun fighters' the Vought F-8 Crusader first flew in 1955 and performed with great success against the MiG's of North Vietnam. As well as being in service with the US Navy and Marine Corps, it operated with the Philippine Air Force and the French Navy. F-8D Crusader 148693 is at the Mid-America Air Museum, Liberal, Kansas.

In 1963, the US Navy initiated a design competition for a replacement for the A-4 Skyhawk in the light attack role. The winner was the Ling-Temco-Vought A-7 Corsair II. The company used the F-8 Crusader as the starting point to re-engineer the type for its new role. The A-7s first flight was in 1965, and the following year the USAF ordered the type as well. A-7D Corsair II 73-1009 is at the Mid-America Air Museum, Kansas.

One of the most stylish of all the carrier-borne aircraft, the North American A-5 Vigilante was conceived as a strategic bomber and then re-tasked as an unarmed reconnaissance aircraft with both photographic and electronic equipment. RA-5C Vigilante 156643 is at the Patuxent River Naval Air Museum, Maryland.

For many years, the North American (later Rockwell) T-2 Buckeye was the advanced training aircraft for the US Navy and Marine Corps. It was in this type that trainee pilots performed their first carrier landings. It has since been replaced by the T-45 Goshawk. T-2C Buckeye 158320 is at the Patuxent River Naval Air Museum.

A delta-wing configured single-seat, carrier-borne fighter, the Douglas F-6A Skyray was the first US Navy interceptor capable of Mach 1 in level flight. F-6A Skyray 134550 is preserved at Oceana NAS, Virginia.

The McDonnell F2H Banshee was a follow-on fighter-bomber development from the earlier FH-1 Phantom I. The first prototype took to the air in January 1949 and deliveries to the US Navy began just three months later. F2H-4 Banshee 127693 is marked as 147369 at Oceana NAS.

First flown in March 1948, the Douglas Skyknight was an all-weather, carrier-borne fighter with side-by-side seating for the pilot and radar operator. It was later to serve as the first tactical jet to take on the electronic warfare role in the US Marine Corps. TF-10B Skyknight 127074 is on the deck of the Intrepid Air-Sea-Space Museum, New York City.

The most high-profile user of the Grumman Tiger was the US Navy Flight Demonstration Squadron *The Blue Angels*. The unit operated the type from 1957 until the end of 1968, when it transitioned to the F-4 Phantom II. F-11A Tiger 141832 is at the Cradle of Aviation Museum, Garden City, New York.

Convair's Sea Dart was a US Navy requirement for a water-based fighter with a large retractable hydro-ski for landing. It first flew in 1953 and the following year passed a speed of Mach 1. It never entered production or service. YF2Y-1 Sea Dart 135765 is on display at the Florida Air Museum, Lakeland.

The North American Fury was a naval version of the F-86 Sabre, first flying in 1951. Many changes had to be made to the original to make the aircraft suitable to operation from aircraft carriers, not the least folding wings. More than 1,000 were delivered to the US Navy and Marine Corps. FJ-4B Fury N400FS is a privately owned and flown example and seen on take-off at Oshkosh, Wisconsin.

With a production run of more than 3,000 airframes, the Douglas Skyhawk served both the US Navy and Marine Corps, as well as the air arms of many other nations. It was a lightweight, carrier-based, single-seat attack-bomber. A-4M Skyhawk 160024 is preserved at the Havelock Tourist & Event Centre, North Carolina.

It may be thought odd that one of the most advanced combat aircraft that is only now joining the air arms of many nations should be in a museum, but when the prototypes are no longer needed, museum retirement may be their fate. Lockheed-Martin X-35B Lightning II 301 can be seen at the National Air and Space Museum, Steven F. Udvar-Hazy Centre, Chantilly, Virginia. The F-35 was the winner of the Joint Strike Fighter competition.

For every winner there has to be a loser and in the Joint Strike Fighter competition that was the fate of the Boeing X-32B. It was perhaps not the most elegant aircraft ever to fly and one of the prototypes is to be found at the Patuxent River Naval Air Museum, Maryland.

To replace the U-2 reconnaissance aircraft, the manufacturer, Lockheed produced the A-12, to be operated by the Central Intelligence Agency (CIA). It first flew in 1962 from the secret Groom Lake site in Nevada and was a single-seat aircraft of still unsurpassed performance. Lockheed A-12 60-6925 is on the deck at the Intrepid Air-Sea-Space Museum aboard the former aircraft carrier USS *Intrepid* (CV-11) in New York City.

Developed from the A-12 for the USAF's reconnaissance needs, the Lockheed Blackbird added a second crew member to operate its many systems. While in service, it broke a number of world speed records that will stand for years to come. It flew from New York to London in 1 hour 54 minutes and London to Los Angeles in 3 hours 47 minutes. SR-71A Blackbird 61-7960 is at the Castle Air Museum, California.

The Lockheed Viking was designed as a carrier-based, anti-submarine, search-and-strike aircraft. It first flew in November 1971 and in service had a crew of four. S-3B Viking 160599 is on the deck of the USS Hornet Air and Sea Museum, Alameda, California.

With a history dating back to 1954 when the contract for production was signed, the Lockheed U-2 was often shrouded in great secrecy. It first flew from Groom Lake in 1955. Its role was to fly over the Soviet Union and, using the most advanced cameras available, photograph strategic sites. Early operations were by the CIA, and later the USAF, which still use the type. U-2D 56-6721 is at the Blackbird Air Park, Palmdale, California.

Not all preserved aircraft have long production runs and history. For some designs, just one model was built because it never achieved its potential. One such is the Beech Jet Mentor. It was built as a private venture using as much as possible from the Beech T-34 Mentor basic trainer. When it first flew in December 1955 there were signs that the US Navy was looking for a primary jet trainer. The idea was later dropped by the navy, which resumed using the T-34. Beech 73 Jet Mentor N134B is at the Kansas Aviation Museum, Wichita.

In October 1947, Captain Charles (Chuck) Yeager flew the rocket-powered Bell X-1 through the sound barrier for the first time, having been dropped from the bomb bay of a B-29. The aircraft was named *Glamourous Glennis* after his wife. Bell X-1 46-062 is on display at the National Air and Space Museum, Washington DC.

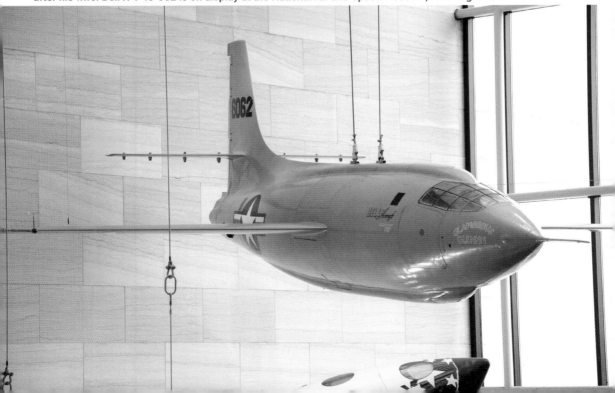

The McDonnell Goblin seemed like a good idea on paper but failed in the real world. This 'parasite fighter' was to be carried by a bomber for its own protection. The idea was not new as it had been used in the 1930s with airships. Post-World War Two, it was thought that the B-36 could carry a Goblin on a retractable trapeze beneath it. It could then be lowered, as needed, and later recovered. However, flight trials proved that it would be very unstable in the recovery mode and the project was cancelled with just two prototypes built. XF-85 Goblin 46-0524 is at the Strategic Air and Space Museum, Ashland, Nebraska.

It is not uncommon for aircraft from many nations to find their way into museums in the USA. One such is the Dassault Etendard. Used by the French Navy as a carrier-based attack and reconnaissance aircraft, it first joined the fleet in 1962 and was later replaced by the Super Etendard and that by the Rafale. Etendard IVM No.60 is on the Intrepid Air-Sea-Space Museum, New York.

Once the standard jet trainer for the air forces of the Warsaw Pact, the Czech-designed and built Aero L-29 Delfin first flew in April 1959. With the collapse of the communist governments in many Eastern European countries, Soviet-era aircraft have become available to western-buyers. L-29 Delphin N129SH is privately owned and pictured competing in the air races at Reno, Nevada.

First flown in November 1968, the Aero L-39 Albatros was a follow-on design to replace the L-29. Nearly 3,000 have been produced and they still serve with more than 20 air forces around the world. It has proved to be a popular jet warbird for private owners in the USA. L-39C Albatros NX139TB is seen on the taxiway at Lakeland, Florida about to depart.

Designed and built in Poland, the PZL Mielec TS-11 Iskra first flew in February 1960. It was hoped to be the aircraft to win the evaluation to be the jet trainer for the Warsaw Pact but lost out to the Aero L-29. The Polish government, wanting to support its own aircraft industry, decided to build it for the Polish Air Force, and it entered service in 1964. These aircraft have also become popular in the private market and TS-11 Iskra N707LC is pictured at the Reno Air Races, Nevada.

The Soviet Union's first operational swept-wing, jet fighter was the Mikoyan and Gurevich MiG-15 (the NATO reporting name for it was Fagot). More than 3,000 airframes have been built and it has served with air forces worldwide. It was licence-built in Poland. Pictured at the Air Power Heritage Park, Fallon NAS, is Polish-built WSK Lim-2 (MiG-15bis) 1614. It is marked as '546' and is in North Korean markings.

Following the MiG-15 was the MiG-17; it entered Soviet service in the early 1950s and carried the NATO reporting name Fresco. Vast numbers were produced – more than 8,000 – and again they were licence-built in Poland. WSK Lim-5 (MiG-17F) 1319 wears Soviet markings of '3020' at the Air Power Heritage Park, Fallon NAS.

The MiG-21 (Fishbed) started life as a simple lightweight fighter and grew into a multi-role machine that can still be found in service with air forces to this day. Early MiG-21F-13 '69' is pictured at the Strategic Air and Space Museum, Nebraska, in the restoration hangar. This aircraft was originally operated by the Indonesian Air Force and believed to have transferred to the USAF in the 'Constant Peg' programme in Nevada during the 1980s. This secret programme involved training regular squadron pilots to fly against opposition aircraft to give them experience of how such an adversary could perform.

A Mach-2, swing-wing, single-seat interceptor, the MiG-23 (Flogger) first flew in June 1967 and entered service in 1970. More than 5,000 airframes have been constructed. MiG-23ML '353' is a former East German example, now wearing Russian markings, at the Air Power Heritage Park, Fallon NAS.

A very able and nimble fighter aircraft, with a Mach-2 performance, the MiG-29 (Fulcrum) is still in frontline service with many air forces of the world. The prototype first flew in October 1977. MiG-29A '15' wears Russian markings at the Air Power Heritage Park, Fallon NAS.

The Aermacchi MB-339 is an Italian-designed-and-built advanced jet trainer that also has the ability to carry underwing weapon stores. Pictured on the deck of the Intrepid Air-Sea-Space Museum, New York, is MB-339A MM54461 in the colours of the *Frecce Tricolori*, the Italian Air Force aerobatic team.

First introduced into Royal Air Force (RAF) service in 1952, the two-seat, side-by-side de Havilland Vampire trainer was developed from the single-seat fighter version that had entered RAF service in 1946. Both variants sold worldwide. Privately owned D.H.115 Vampire T.55 N115DH wears Royal Navy markings at Reno, Nevada, where it was flying in the annual races. The serial reference – XG775 – and the colour scheme belong to another airframe; this aircraft was once with the Swiss Air Force.

First flown in July 1955, the Folland Gnat was perhaps the smallest lightweight fighter to enter service. It served with the Finnish Air Force and was manufactured in India and whilst in service with the Indian Air Force saw conflicts with Pakistan. A two-seat advanced trainer version served with the RAF. Gnat F1 E1222, in Indian markings, is at the Mid-American Air Museum, Liberal, Kansas.

The Hunting (BAe) Jet Provost was the standard jet trainer for the RAF for many years until it was replaced by the Short-built Tucano. Many have been sold to private users. Jet Provost T.5 N287XW, still in its RAF livery, is pictured flying at Oshkosh, Wisconsin.

The Gloster Meteor entered RAF service in 1944 as its first jet fighter. It was 1948 before the two-seat variant flew, and it joined as an advance trainer the following year. This version did not have ejector seats. The Meteor was sold in large numbers worldwide. Meteor T.7 N313Q is seen taking off at Oshkosh, Wisconsin, and was privately owned. It has since joined the Planes of Fame Museum at Chino, California.

Hawker's P.1127 proved to be the first practical vertical take-off-and-landing (VTOL) aircraft. This was thanks to the use of a single engine with moveable nozzles to transit from vertical to forward flight. It first flew in 1960, and in 1964 a development named the Kestrel was operated by a unit jointly funded by the British, German and American governments. This was known as the Tripartite Evaluation Squadron with pilots from all three nations. Following the trials, the aircraft were offered to each of the countries for further tests. In the USA, NASA operated them for some years. P.1127 Kestrel (XV-6A) NASA 521 is at the Virginia Air and Space Centre at Hampton.

After the Kestrel came the operational Harrier, this was followed by an improved version with a bigger wing. McDonnell Douglas/British Aerospace AV-8B Harrier II 162969 is on the gate at Cherry Point MCAS, North Carolina.

One of the most amazing privately owned aircraft is BAe Sea Harrier FRS Mk.2 N94422. The type is the dedicated naval version of the Harrier. It is pictured hovering at Oshkosh, Wisconsin.

Designed and built by Avro Canada, the CF-100 was a two-seat, all-weather fighter. As well as service in its native country, it was also operated by the Belgian Air Force. CF-100 Canuck 18152 is at the Bomber Command Museum of Canada, Nanton, Alberta.

The Avro Vulcan was one of a trio of V-bombers to see service with the RAF. It flew active operations in its final years of service during the 1982 Falkland Island conflict. The first deliveries to the RAF, of the B.1, were in 1957 with the B.2 following three years later. Vulcan B.2 XM605 is at the Castle Air Museum, Atwater, California.

From its first flight in 1949, the English Electric Canberra proved to be one of the most versatile aircraft of all time. It was so good that the USAF bought it and it was licence-built in the USA by the Glen L. Marin Company of Baltimore. Martin RB-57A Canberra 52-1480 is preserved at the Museum of the Kansas National Guard, Topeka.

Conceived to be a jack-of-all-trades, the General Dynamics F-111 had a troubled and controversial start to its career. It later matured to be a successful tactical bomber. The SAC of the USAF operated a version with longer-span wings for extra range. FB-111A 68-0267 is at the Strategic Air and Space Museum, Ashland, Nebraska.

A straight-wing, four-engine, tactical-bomber, the North American B-45 Tornado first flew in 1947 and was America's first four-jet bomber. The engines were in paired nacelles under each wing. B-45A Tornado 47-0008 is on show at the Castle Air Museum, California.

Everything about the Convair B-36 bomber is big. It could carry a bomb load of 72,000lb (32,659kg) and had a maximum range of 8,000 miles (12,874km) added to this, it had ten engines. There were six piston powerplants with pusher propellers, which these were augmented with four jets in two pairs under each wing. RB-36H 51-13730 is the largest aircraft at the Castle Air Museum.

Developed from the cancelled Rockwell B-1A bomber, the B-1B was ordered by President Reagan to enhance the power of SAC. The first production aircraft flew in October 1984, with deliveries beginning the following July. It is still in front-line service with the USAF. B-1B Lancer 83-0068 is preserved at the Reflections of Freedom Historic Air Park, McConnell AFB, Kansas.

First flown in 1947, the Boeing B-47 Stratojet was a six-engine bomber. It entered service in 1951 and was retired by the end of the 1960s. B-47E Stratojet 53-4213, like the B-1B, is at McConnell AFB.

The eight-engine Boeing B-52 Stratofortress first took to the air in 1952 and entered service with the USAF three years later. It is still in front-line operational use and there seems to be no plans to retire the aircraft. As well as the USAF, NASA has used the type as the 'mother plane' for a number of the X-series of rocket aircraft. Now retired, NB-52B Stratofortress 52-0008 is at the north gate at Edwards AFB, California. The pylon under the wing that the X-planes were carried aloft in is clearly visible.

The Convair B-58 Hustler was SAC's first supersonic bomber. With a crew of three, it had a maximum speed of 1,385mph (2,229km/hr) and a service ceiling of 63,000ft (19,202m). Its operation life was very short, lasting from 1960 to 1970. TB-58A Hustler 55-0663 is at the Grissom Air Museum, Peru, Indiana.

Designed in the late 1950s and flown in 1963, the six-engine, Mach-3+ North American XB-70 Valkyrie is one of the most futuristic looking bombers ever built. Only two were produced, as it was believed it would not survive if flown over the Soviet Union due to the development of that country's surface-to-air missiles. The sole surviving XB-70 62-001 is at the National Museum of the USAF, Dayton, Ohio.

The most widely used advanced training aircraft has to be the North American T-6 Texan. It was also known in US Navy service as the SNJ and in many other air arms as the Harvard. It could still be found in operation with the South African Air Force as late as the 1990s. There are literally hundreds flying in private ownership, or preserved in museums around the world. It was licence-built in Canada, first by Noorduyn and then, from 1951, by the Canadian Car & Foundry Company. Harvard Mk. IV N7522U is seen at the Reno races and was built by the latter company.

In its role as a basic trainer, the North American T-28 Trojan first entered service with the USAF and then later with the US Navy. It was also widely exported. T-28C Trojan N2215D is a privately owned example seen on the move at Lakeland, Florida.

Not all preserved aircraft have long and illustrious histories and that did not achieve fame also deserve a degree of preservation. One such is the North American O-47B. It was single-engine, observation aircraft powered by a 975hp Wright R-1820 radial piston engine. It first flew in 1938 and its service life was in second-line duties. O-47B N73716 is at the Combat Air Museum, Topeka, Kansas.

The Curtiss P-40 was to be found on almost every front during World War Two. Its production figures were only beaten by the P-51 and P-47. It is a popular warbird for the private user. One such is P-40E Warhawk N2416X seen landing at Oshkosh, Wisconsin.

The number of North American P-51 Mustangs that are preserved in museums and still flying tops the warbird fighter lists. As soon as the Rolls-Royce Merlin engine was fitted to the original airframe it became the fighter that could escort the United States Army Air Force's (USAAF) bombers as far as Berlin and back. Operated by the Military Aircraft Museum, P-51D Mustang N51EA takes off from its base at Virginia Beach Airport.

With the North American Mustang being available in reasonable numbers, some airframes have been converted to race in the unlimited category at Reno, Nevada. It is the world's fastest motorsport. P-51D Mustang N11FT named *Strega* is one such conversion. Note the way the canopy has been cut down in size to reduce drag. This privately owned example first won at Reno in 1987 and has repeated the feat several times since then. It is pictured at Reno.

More than 15,000 Republic P-47 Thunderbolts were produced. The aircraft was the largest single-seat, single-engine fighter of World War Two. It served in the USA with the National Guard units until as late as 1955. Fewer are to be found flying compared to other contemporary aircraft. Owned by the Erickson Aircraft Collection, Madras, Oregon and pictured at Chino, California is P-47D Thunderbolt NX47DA.

A direct development from the earlier Bell P-39 Airacobra, the P-63 Kingcobra retained the earlier aircraft's design feature of having the engine positioned behind the pilot as well as an actual door to enter the cockpit. As with both types, vast amounts of the production were shipped to the Soviet Union. It is perhaps the rarest of the flying warbirds. P-63A Kingcobra NX191H is operated by the Commemorative Air Force from its Peachtree, Georgia chapter and is pictured at Virginia Beach Airport.

The Grumman F4F Wildcat was the first of that manufacturer's line of monoplane fighters for the US Navy. During World War Two, vast numbers of fighters were needed so more companies set up production lines. General Motors produced the Wildcat under the designation FM-2. Pictured at Reno, Nevada is privately owned FM-2 Wildcat N86572.

One of the most widely used torpedo-bombers of World War Two, the Grumman (TBM) Avenger was a carrier-borne aircraft with a crew of three. Privately owned TBM Avenger N3969A is pictured visiting Cherry Point MCAS, North Carolina. This airframe survived because was it was used as a water bomber in Canada until well into the 1990s.

Vought's F4U Corsair was the finest of the US Navy and Marine Corps single-seat fighters of World War Two. Still in service during the Korean War (1950–53), it soldiered on in South and Central America into the late 1960s. It was distinctive, with its inverted gull-wings to keep the undercarriage short while allowing for a powerful engine. F4U-4 Corsair 97369 is on display at the National Museum of the Marine Corps, Triangle, Virginia.

The US Navy's principal carrier-based dive-bomber during World War Two was the Douglas Dauntless. Pictured at Fond du Lac, Wisconsin, is SBD-4S Dauntless NL826A owned by the Commemorative Air Force, where pleasure flights were being offered to the public.

Operational with the US Navy from 1943, the Curtiss Helldiver was a two-crew, carrier-based bomber. Operated by the Commemorative Air Force SB2C-5 Helldiver N92879 is on the move at Oshkosh, Wisconsin.

The Douglas Skyraider provided the US military with one of its most versatile aircraft. Original operations were with the navy as a ground attack bomber and even, in other versions, as an airborne early-warning platform. It was later used by the air force during the Vietnam War, supporting helicopters that flew into North Vietnam to rescue pilots who had been shot down. AD-4B Skyraider 132261 is preserved at the Air Power Heritage Park, Fallon NAS, Nevada.

The last of the Grumman single-engine, piston-powered fighters for the US Navy was the F8F Bearcat. It was too late for World War Two but saw action with the French in Indochina (1946–54). Two civil variants were made with the designation G.58. One was for Gulf Oil and the other was retained by the manufacturer as a demonstrator. This one, G-58B Bearcat NL700A now wears military markings and is pictured at the Palm Springs Air Museum, California.

First flown in May 1950, the Douglas Skyshark was a turboprop attack bomber designed as a possible replacement for the still-very-new Skyraider. Although it had a better performance in several key aspects, it was let down by numerous problems with the powerplant and the project was terminated. A2D Skyshark 125485 is owned by the San Diego Aerospace Museum and is at Gillespie Field, the museum's second site and storage unit.

One of the most important British warplanes of all time was the Hawker Hurricane. During the Battle of Britain, it shot down more enemy aircraft than its contemporary, the Spitfire. Hurricane Mk.XII N943HH is operated by the Military Aircraft Museum at Virginia Beach.

The Supermarine Spitfire was in front-line service with the RAF as a fighter from the start to the end of World War Two. The engine power grew from the 1,030hp Rolls-Royce Merlin of the Mk. 1 to the 2,050hp Griffon of the Mk. 24. Spitfire Mk. IXe C-GYQQ is a privately owned example seen flying at Oshkosh, Wisconsin.

The Royal Navy's last single-engine, piston-powered fighter was the Hawker Sea Fury. It served on the front-line from 1947 for seven years, and during the Korean War shot down a MiG-15. It is a popular racing machine as a stock aircraft it is fast, but when fitted with a Pratt & Whitney R-4360 engine it is capable of winning the unlimited class at the Reno races. Sea Fury FB.11 NX15S is operated by the Commemorative Air Force and is pictured on take-off at Oshkosh, Wisconsin.

The original role of the Westland Lysander was that of an army co-operation aircraft but during World War Two it played an important role by using its short take-off and landing performance. It was used to transport agents into enemy-occupied France landing in fields at night, which were lit only by torch light. It was also licence-built in Canada where one of its roles was as a target-tug. Lysander Mk. IIIA C-GCWL wears the high-visibility colour scheme associated with this task. It is owned by the Canadian Warplane Heritage Museum, Mount Hope, Ontario.

The Polikarpov I-153 was the final member of the biplane range of fighters from that manufacturer. It was similar to the I-15, but developments included a retractable undercarriage. The I-153 Chaika (Seagull) first flew in 1938. N153RP is part of the Military Aircraft Museum at Virginia Beach and was rebuilt in New Zealand from the parts of other airframes.

First flown in 1933, the Polikarpov I-16 was the first of the monoplane fighters from the company. It was used in action during the Spanish Civil War (1936–39). I-16 Rata N1639P is to be found at the Military Aircraft Museum, Virginia Beach.

Yakovlev Yak-3UA NX854DP was built by the Yakovlev company in 1993. It proved to be an amazing comeback for a World War Two fighter but there was a demand from American collectors for flying warbirds, and so the original manufacturer built a batch with a gap of 40 plus years in the production line. They were, however, fitted with an American in-line engine. This aircraft is privately owned and pictured at Reno, Nevada.

This Yak-3U N46463 was built in Romania by the Avioane Aircraft Company, in 2005, to the specification of the Yak-11 trainer. Now, however it was fitted with a Pratt & Whitney R-2000 radial engine. It is pictured at Reno, Nevada but has since been sold in Australia and re-registered.

Developed from the MiG-1, the MiG-3 was one of the first designs from that design bureaux, and the company almost exclusively built fighters. MiG-3 N107FB is owned by the Military Aircraft Museum and pictured at its workshop at Suffolk County Airport, Virginia. This airframe was rebuilt, in Russia, from several wrecks.

The Messerschmitt Bf-109 was the best know fighter used by the Luftwaffe during World War Two. It was built in very large numbers. Bf-109G-4 N109GY, owned by the Military Aircraft Museum, is pictured ready to fly at its Virginia Beach base. This aircraft was rebuilt from a crashed example found in Russia.

Designed by Kurt Tank, the Focke-Wulf Fw-190 entered Luftwaffe service in late 1941 and outclassed all other fighters at that time. Fw-190A-8 N447FW is now owned by the Erickson Aircraft Collection, Madras, Oregon, and pictured at Virginia Beach.

A remarkable shape and with a performance to match, the Dornier Do-335 Pfeil (Arrow) had engines at each end of the fuselage, one to pull and one to push. It first flew in October 1943 and could reach a speed of 474mph (763km/hr). Like so many advanced German aircraft, at that time, there were too few and it was manufactured too late to change the course of the war. Do-335A-1 VG+PH is at the National Air and Space Museum, Chantilly, Virginia.

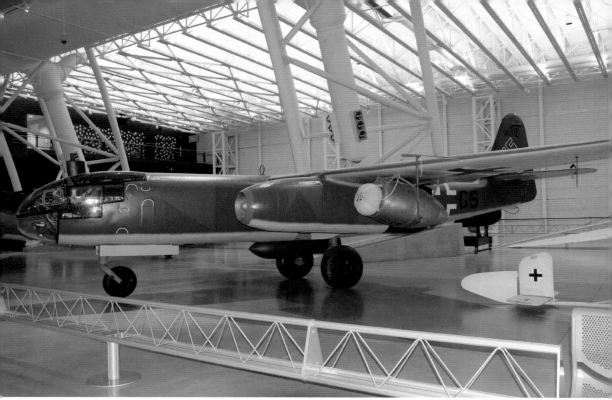

The world's first jet bomber, the Arado Ar-234 Blitz (Lightning) first flew in June 1943. Despite being designed as a bomber, its main operational role was as a photo-reconnaissance platform as its performance made it difficult to intercept. Ar-234B-2 FI+GS is at the National Air and Space Museum, Virginia.

Before it could fly its first operational mission, World War Two had ended. However, the Aichi M6A Seiran (Mountain Haze) was the first submarine-borne aircraft for attack missions. Two aircraft were to be housed in a large hangar with a catapult on the forward deck. The Seiran had a complicated system to fold the wing and tail to fit the space available. M6A-1 Seiran 47 is at the National Air and Space Museum, Virginia.

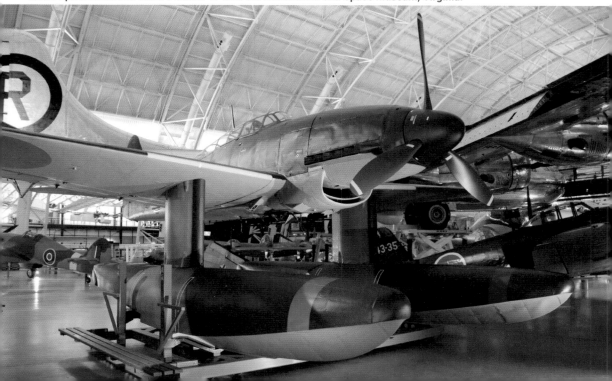

A long-range, twin-engine escort or night fighter, the Nakajima J1N1-S Gekko (Moonlight) had a pair of fuselage-mounted 20mm cannons that fired upwards. The plan was to fly under the target and destroy it without being seen, this was, of course, in its night-fighting role. J1N1-S Gekko 7334 is at the National Air and Space Museum, Virginia.

The best known of the Japanese aircraft of the Pacific War (1941–45) was the Mitsubishi A6M Reisen (Zero). It operated throughout the entire conflict. The only original flying example, with its original engine, is A6M5 Zero NX46770 operated by the Planes of Fame Air Museum, Chino, California.

The Lockheed Lightning had the most distinctive shape of all the operational aircraft built in America during World War Two. It was a twin-boom, twin-engine, single-seat fighter. P-38J Lightning NX138AM is operated by the Planes of Fame Air Museum at Chino.

First flown in November 1943, the Grumman Tigercat was designed for the US Navy as a twin-engine, carrier-borne fighter. It did not have great success as a ship-based aircraft and was more successful when flown from land bases. Post-war, a number were used as water bombers until the early 1980s and these have provided the stock for the current flying examples. F7F-3P Tigercat NX700F is privately owned and pictured at Reno, Nevada.

The most versatile piston-engined warplane ever, the de Havilland Mosquito operated in fighter, bomber, reconnaissance and many other roles. It stayed in RAF service, in second-line duties, until the early 1960s. Following the loss, in 1996, of the BAe-operated one, it was some years before another Mosquito flew. In New Zealand, a number have since been restored to flying condition. The first of these, in September 2012, was sold to the Military Aircraft Museum. D.H.98 Mosquito FB.26 N114KA is pictured on the move at its Virginia Beach base.

First flown in 1942, in the role of a light bomber, the Douglas A-26/B-26 Invader has taken part in a trio of wars for the Americans; World War Two (1941–45), Korea (1950–53) and Vietnam (1961–73), as well as seeing action for other nations. One such was the Bay of Pigs invasion (16–20 April 1961) of Cuba when it was operated by both sides. Pictured as a memorial to those killed trying to overthrow the Castro government. is this A-26C Invader at the Liberation Air Force Memorial, Tamiami, Florida. It wears false Cuban marks of '931' and was the former Canadian water bomber C-FMSB.

One of the most widely used light bombers of World War Two was the North American B-25 Mitchell. Its most famous single operation was the first bombing raid on Japan when the US Army Air Force flew from the carrier USS *Hornet*, in April 1942. TB-25K Mitchell N27493 is owned by the Commemorative Air Force and is pictured at Virginia Beach giving pleasure flights to the public.

Serving for the whole of World War Two, the Boeing B-17 Flying Fortress to many people in the USA, sums up the bombing offensive in that conflict. B-17G Flying Fortress N3193G, named *Yankee Lady*, is operated by the Yankee Air Force Museum at Willow Run Airport, Michigan. It is pictured at Farmingdale, New York. This aircraft had been a water bomber until 1986 and prior to that appeared in the film *Tora! Tora! Tora!*

This Boeing B-29 Superfortress flew into the history books when it dropped the first atom bomb on Hiroshima in August 1945. B-29 Superfortress 44-86292, named *Enola Gay* after the pilot's mother, is at the National Air and Space Museum, Virginia.

Only two Boeing B-29 Superfortress bombers are currently airworthy. It was the aircraft that bore the brunt of the attacks on the Japanese mainland during the Pacific War. It also flew missions during the war in Korea. Taking off from Oshkosh, Wisconsin, is TB-29 Superfortress N69972 named *Doc*. It is operated from its base in Wichita, Kansas.

By the side of the B-17s, over Europe, was the Consolidated B-24 Liberator. Far fewer survive than the B-17. One that still takes to the air is operated by the Commemorative Air Force. LB-30 Liberator 1 N24927 is pictured visiting Oshkosh, Wisconsin. The LB-30 was the transport version of the type.

The Consolidated PB4Y Privateer was the maritime patrol version of the B-24. The single tall fin was the main recognition difference. The type served as water bombers until as late as 2003. Arizona-based PB4Y-2G Privateer N2871G is pictured flying at Chino, California.

There are many aircraft types that served in conflicts with no examples preserved. To restore that balance, some airframes have literally been dragged from the sea for restoration. One such is the Handley Page Hampden. This aircraft, P5436, was ditched while on a training flight in Canada and was later restored and exhibited. It can be seen at the Canadian Museum of Flight, Langley, British Colombia.

Another World War Two bomber that has been salvaged following a ditching is Handley Page Halifax Mk. VIIA NA337. It was shot down on a mission to drop supplies to the Norwegian resistance in April 1945 and ditched in Lake Mjøsa. Fifty years later, it was lifted out and taken to Canada for restoration. It is pictured, prior to painting, at the National Air Force Museum of Canada, Trenton, Ontario. Many Canadian squadrons of RAF Bomber Command flew the Halifax.

Of the thousands of Avro Lancaster bombers that once flew, only two are currently airworthy; one is in the UK, and the other is with the Canadian Warplane Heritage Museum, Mount Hope, Ontario. This aircraft Lancaster 10(MA) C-GVRA is pictured at the museum's base giving pleasure flights to members.

The most widely used transport aircraft of the Luftwaffe during World War Two was the three-engined Junkers Ju-52/3m. A few genuine ones exist, but most of the flying examples are the Spanish, licence-built version, the CASA 352, and many of these now wear Luftwaffe markings. CASA 352 (Ju-52/3m) N352JU is pictured crew training at Virginia Beach, where it is owned by the Military Aircraft Museum.

First flown in June 1937, the Lockheed 12 Electra Junior was designed as a business aircraft or a feed-liner, feeding passengers from small airports to larger ones to connect to long-distance services. 12A Electra Junior NC2072, a privately owned example, is pictured arriving at Oshkosh, Wisconsin.

It is a noticeable fact that far fewer civil airliner types are preserved than military ones. It is good to see some examples that buck this trend. The Martin 4-0-4 was a post-war, piston-engined airliner and had a similar configuration to the Convair 240. Martin 4-0-4 N450A is in the livery of Eastern Air Lines and preserved by the Mid-Atlantic Air Museum, Reading, Pennsylvania.

One of the great successes of the post-war British aviation industry was the Vickers Viscount. It sold worldwide following its first flight in 1948. It was the first four-engine turboprop airliner to enter service. Viscount V.757 C-FTHG is at the British Colombia Aviation Museum at Sidney, having spent many years at a mechanics' training school at nearby Vancouver.

Only one successful supersonic airliner was able to operate regular passenger services at speeds and heights that may never be equalled. The BAe/Aérospatiale Concorde was the ultimate head turner at the airports it flew from. In October 2003, British Airways took the type out of service. Preserved next to the Intrepid Air-Sea-Space Museum is Concorde 102 G-BOAD. It is ironic for New York to want to display an aircraft type that the city fought so hard to stop ever landing there.

Still to be found operating on wheels/skis/floats in remote parts of the world, the de Havilland Canada Beaver is one of the finest utility aircraft ever built. Preserved at the 45th Infantry Division Museum, Oklahoma City is DHC-2 (U-6A) Beaver 56-0367. The US Army operated more than 600 examples of the type.

Another aircraft used in large numbers by the US Army was the Cessna O-1 Bird Dog with nearly 3,000 being purchased. Its roles included liaison, observation and flight training. O-1A Bird Dog 51-4651 is at the 45th Infantry Division Museum.

The Cessna 310 twin-engine cabin monoplane first flew in 1954 and was ordered off-the-shelf by the USAF with a number being transferred to the US Army. Its roles included utility and staff transport. U-3A Blue Canoe 58-2166 is at the 45th Infantry Division Museum.

Designed to meet a US Marine Corps requirement for a purpose-built Counter Insurgency (COIN) aircraft, the North American (Later Rockwell) OV-10 Bronco was built. The first prototype flew in July 1965. Production aircraft also served with the USAF in the forward air control role. It was also exported to a number of nations. Pictured at the Mid-America Air Museum, Liberal, Kansas, is YOV-10A Bronco 152880.

Based upon the Bristol Britannia but without the pressurisation, and piston engines in place of turboprops, the Canadair CL-28 Argus was a maritime patrol aircraft operated only by the Royal Canadian Air Force (RCAF). The prototype first flew in March 1957 and the type remained in service until 1981. CP-107 Argus 2 10742 is at Canada's Aviation and Space Museum, Ottawa, Ontario.

The Lockheed C-141 Starlifter jet first flew in December 1963 and gave the USAF a large capacity, long-range and fast transport to replace the slow piston-powered C-124 Globemaster II. In the following decade, almost all the fleet was stretched by 23ft 4in (7.11m) to give 30 per cent more cargo space. One of the few not converted was C-141A Starlifter 61-2775. It is on show at the Air Mobility Command Museum, Dover AFB, Delaware.

Lockheed's C-5 Galaxy is the largest transport aircraft in current service with the USAF. It first flew in June 1968, and deliveries began at the end of the following year. C-5A Galaxy 69-0014 is at the Air Mobility Command Museum.

The Douglas C-133 Cargomaster first flew in 1956. Its role was as a heavy strategic, turboprop-powered transport aircraft. One of its design features was that it could carry an Intercontinental Ballistic Missile (ICBM) such as the Thor, this being loaded through the large rear freight door. The fleet was withdrawn from service in the early 1970s. C-133B Cargomaster 59-0536 is at the Air Mobility Command Museum.

The second of three aircraft to have the name Globemaster, the Douglas C-124 was a heavy, strategic, piston-powered transport with two decks inside the fuselage. C-124A Globemaster II 49-0258 is at the Air Mobility Command Museum.

The latest aircraft with the Globemaster name is the McDonnell Douglas C-17. The prototype first took to the air in September 1991, and deliveries began two years later. It remains in full service with the USAF and has also been sold to a number of other air forces. C-17A Globemaster III 87-0025, one of the early airframes, is preserved at the National Museum of the USAF, Dayton, Ohio.

A twin-boom, twin-engine troop and freight transport, the Fairchild C-119 Flying Boxcar served the USAF in the conflicts of Korea and Vietnam, in the latter it operated as a gunship. C-119F Flying Boxcar N3559 is painted as '0-12881' at the Air Mobility Command Museum. This airframe, in fact, served in Canada with the RCAF and then the USA as a civilian water bomber.

The Boeing C-135 Stratotanker airframes have provided the USAF with an endless supply of sub-variants to carry out many different roles. EC-135K 55-3118 is preserved at the Reflections of Freedom Air Park, McConnell AFB, Kansas. This version, one of just three being converted, were to provide accurate navigation information to fighters as they accompanied them on deployments to Europe or Asia.

With sales of 1,832, the Boeing 727 was the world's best-selling airliner until it was overtaken by its baby brother, the 737, and then by the Airbus A320 range. One of the largest users of the type was the parcel delivery giant Federal Express. As the company retired the tri-jet, some have found their way into museums, or colleges to train engineers. Boeing 727-173C N199FE is preserved at the Kansas Aviation Museum, Wichita.

The Boeing 737 has gone from the -100 to -900 and the new MAX variants, as well as the military and business jet versions, and is still in full production. A few old -200s are still to found in service. Boeing 737-2H4 N29SW is preserved at the Kansas Aviation Museum.

An aircraft that truly changed flying was the Boeing 747, also known as the jumbo jet. The recent COVID-19 pandemic has caused some airlines to retire their fleets prematurely, but 747s will fly for many more years in the cargo role. One of the small number preserved so far is Boeing 747SR-46 N911NA. It was used by NASA to carry the now-retired Space Shuttle from its landing site at Edwards AFB, California, to the launch platform in Florida. Note the fastening locations on the top of the fuselage and the endplates on the tail. It is to be seen at the Joe Davis Heritage Air Park, Palmdale, California.

One of the most stylish and high-performance business jets is the Gates (now Bombardier) Learjet. The early short-body ones had a fighter-like climb rate. Few private jets get preserved, so it is good to see Learjet 23 N505PF at the Kansas Aviation Museum.

Used by the US military as a VIP transport or pilot/radar-operator trainer, the North American Sabreliner was also used as a business jet in the civil market. T-39D Sabreliner 150987 was operated by the US Navy Test Pilots School and features an extended nose. It is pictured at the Patuxent River Naval Air Museum, Maryland.

The current carrier-based, airborne, early-warning aircraft with the US Navy is the Grumman E-2 Hawkeye. It entered service in 1964 and over the years has been continually updated to enhance its capability. It is distinguished by a large rotodome housing the radar that rotates at six revolutions per minute. E-2C Hawkeye 165300 is on display at Ely Memorial Park, Norfolk Naval Air Station (NAS), Virginia.

The first of the Canadian-built STOL twin-engined aircraft, the de Havilland Canada DHC-4 Caribou, first flew in July 1958. Its ability to operate into and out of short unprepared strips has made it a difficult aircraft to replace. In the colours of the Golden Knights, the US Army parachute team, is DHC-4 (YAC-1) Caribou 57-3079 pictured at the US Army Transportation Museum, Fort Eustis, Virginia.

That most elegant of airliners, the Lockheed Constellation had a role to play in the US military. As well as a transport aircraft, it had an airborne early-warning variant. EC-121T Super Constellation 52-3418 is at the Combat Air Museum, Topeka, Kansas. Note the under-fuselage bulge housing the radar.

Ordered first as a navigation trainer, then as a general transport aircraft, the Convair T-29 was a military version of the post-war Convair 240 airliner. Re-engined and stretched versions are still to be found in civil operations. Pictured in the restoration hangar at the Strategic Air and Space Museum, Ashland, Nebraska, is Convair T-29A 50-0190.

The most modern airliner of its day, the Boeing 307 Stratoliner had four engines and a pressurised cabin. It first flew in 1938. The last one to fly was stored in Arizona for many years before being restored by Boeing in Seattle. That organisation flew it to the National Air and Space Museum in Virginia. B307 N19903 wears period Pan American markings as well as a highly polished finish.

Dating back to 1933, the Boeing 247 was one of the first all-metal monoplane airliners. B247D NC13369 hangs on display at the National Air and Space Museum at the Washington DC site.

From the late 1940s until the early 1960s, the Lockheed P2V Neptune was the US Navy's frontline maritime patrol aircraft. The type also served with the air arms of other nations until much later. In the USA, the Neptune found a new role as a water bomber protecting the nation's forests. They were retired from this task as late as 2017. P2V-7 (SP-2H) Neptune N443NA was one of these and was delivered to the San Diego Air and Space Museum at its storage base at Gillespie Field, in September 2018.

The military variant of the Boeing 377 Stratocruiser preceded the civil airliner by three years. The largest batch were built as flying tankers to refuel in-flight the bombers of the USAF's SAC. The last version had a pair of J47 jets added under the wings to enable the tanker to match the speed needed to refuel jets. Pictured at the Air Mobility Command Museum, Delaware, is Boeing KC-97L 53-0230.

The last of the great propliners from Douglas, the DC-7 first flew in 1953. In only a few years it was supplanted by the early jets and turboprops. However, it did have a long life flying for holiday charter airlines and as a water bomber. The last of these was not retired until October 2020. Pictured on the move at Oshkosh, Wisconsin, is Douglas DC-7B N836D. After a long period of storage, it was restored to flying condition in 2009 and took passengers on pleasure flights. It is currently with the Carolinas Aviation Museum in Charlotte, North Carolina, awaiting an engine repair.

A tactical transport with a short-field performance, the Fairchild C-123 Provider was developed from a transport glider, the Chase XG-20. In its powered form it first flew in October 1949. Later variants had a pair of J85 turbojets, one fitted under each wing to boost performance. During the Vietnam War, 34 airframes were converted with spray bars under the wing; and designated UC-123K. The role of these was to fly over the dense jungle and spray the highly toxic Agent Orange to defoliate the trees and thus deny the Vietcong its cover. UC-123K Provider 54-0658 is at the Air Mobility Command Museum.

The first of the four-engine Douglas airliners was the DC-4 Skymaster. It first flew in 1942, and because of the war, all the early production were the military C-54 version. C-54E Skymaster 44-0930 is at the Air Mobility Command Museum.

The DC-4 was produced under licence in Canada. Unlike the US-built aircraft, it had a pressurised cabin, and the engines were changed to the Rolls-Royce Merlin. It was known as the Canadair C-4 North Star. Pictured at Canada's Aviation and Space Museum, Ottawa is C-4 North Star 17515.

From its first flight in 1935, the Douglas DC-3/C-47 has proved to be impossible to replace. Many modern turboprops were designed to take on that role and failed to do so. The only replacement for a DC-3 has been another DC-3. They still operate scheduled passenger services to this day. Pictured at the National Air Force Museum of Canada, Trenton, Ontario, is C-47 Dakota III 12963.

Hawkair Aviation was the operator of the last commercial service for the Bristol 170 Mk.31M Freighter. The type first flew in 1945 and sold to both civil and military operators worldwide. The twin-nose doors had a wide opening that made loading easy. For many years, the Bristol Freighter operated car-ferry services across the English Channel and the Irish Sea. The last flight by one, was B170 Freighter Mk.31M C-GYQS, which flew to the Reynolds Alberta Museum, Wetaskiwin.

Manufactured by Short Bros, the S.45 Solent was developed from the Seaford flying boat. Wearing period BOAC markings is S.45 Solent N9946F. It has its original British registration of 'G-AKNP' applied. It is pictured at the Oakland Aviation Museum, California.

Based upon the DC-2, the Douglas B-18 Bolo was a pre-war medium bomber. It had a brief frontline service but after the war started, it was relegated to second-line duties. B-18B Bolo 37-029 is at the Castle Air Museum, Atwater, California.

Despite having the same general layout as the C-47, the Curtiss C-46 Commando is a much larger and heavier aircraft. The two types had the same role of cargo and troop transport. A small number still earn their living in Alaska and the far north of Canada. C-46F Commando N78774 named *Tinker Belle* is operated by the Warriors and Warbirds Museum, Munroe, North Carolina, and is pictured landing at Virginia Beach for an air show.

The most widely produced flying boat ever, the Consolidated PBY Catalina, first flew in 1935. It served with many air arms around the world and was licence-built in Canada. One such aircraft is Canadian Vickers PBV-1A Canso N427CV. It is pictured flying, for private owners, at Oshkosh, Wisconsin.

The Ford Tri-Motor dates back to 1926 and was one of the first successful commercial airliners in America. Ford 5-AT-C NC8419 is pictured at Oshkosh, giving pleasure flights. It is operated by the Kalamazoo Air Zoo, Michigan.

Grumman produced a line of four amphibians, in four different sizes. Examples of all are to be found still flying for private owners or in museums. The smallest was the G.44 Widgeon. It first flew in June 1940. Pictured arriving at Oshkosh is G.44A Widgeon N444M.

The next Grumman amphibian, in size, was the G.21 Goose. However, it was an earlier design than the Widgeon, dating back to May 1937. Preserved at the Historic Aircraft Restoration Project, Floyd Bennett Field, New York, is G.21A Goose N644R.

The third of the Grumman amphibians was the post-war G.73 Mallard. It first flew in April 1946. Privately owned G.73 Mallard N98BS is pictured at Lakeland, Florida.

The last and largest of the Grumman amphibians is the HU-16 Albatross. It first flew in October 1947 and was widely used by the US military, as well as many air arms around the world. Pictured at Carson City, Nevada, is privately owned HU-16 Albatross N7025N.

A ten-seat, tri-engined airliner, the Stinson SM 6000B first carried passengers in September 1930, on a service between New York and Washington DC. Only two survive. Pictured in period American Airlines colours, at Oshkosh, is privately owned SM 6000B NC11153.

Introduced in 1934, the Avro 643 Cadet was an improved version of the earlier 631 Cadet; its role was as an ab initio trainer. Australia's air force was one of the customers and it kept its fleet until 1946. Preserved at the Fantasy of Flight Museum, Polk City, Florida, is Avro 643 Cadet II N643AV, still wearing its former Australian livery.

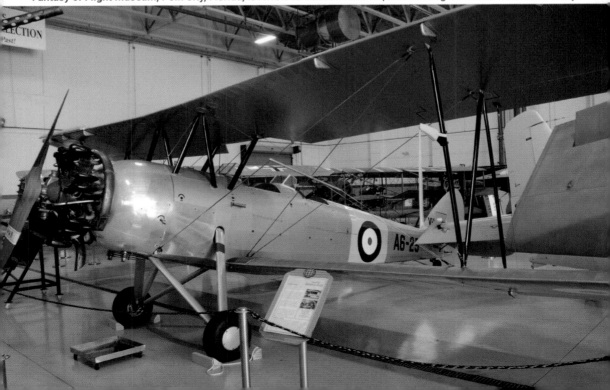

The Vultee BT-13 Valiant first flew in 1939. It was a two-seat, tandem basic trainer with a radial piston engine. One of the many BT-13 Valiant's in private hands, N57486 is seen landing at Oshkosh.

The Cessna 195 Business Liner was a five-seat cabin, touring aircraft with a high wing. More than 1,000 airframes were produced between 1947 and 1954. Privately owned, Cessna 195B N195CW, is pictured on the move at Oshkosh.

First produced in 1932, the Beech 17 Staggerwing is a four-seat biplane with a retractable undercarriage. Despite their age, they command a high price in the second-hand marketplace. Privately owned Beech D17S NC18575 is pictured landing at Oshkosh.

Developed from the earlier Model 3, the Stearman 4 had a more powerful engine and a deeper fuselage. Following its first flight in 1930, one of its main roles was the carriage of mail. Privately owned, Stearman 4E Speedmail NC785H is pictured at Robbinsville, New Jersey.

The first monoplane basic trainer used by the US Army Air Corps was the Ryan YPT-16. It was developed from the civil STA model. Privately owned YPT-16 NC18922 is in its hangar at Robbinsville, New Jersey.

In production from 1928 to 1959, the Polikarpov Po-2 had a production run of some 33,000 airframes. With so many built, it had a legion of roles from basic training, glider-towing to light attack. During World War Two, they were often flown by women pilots in night operations dropping light bombs on German positions to keep them awake. Polikarpov Po-2 N3602 is operated by the Military Aircraft Museum and is pictured at its Suffolk County Airport, Virginia site.

Belgian-designed, the Stampe SV-4 has been produced in its home country as well as in France. It first flew in 1933 and is a two-seat basic trainer. Privately owned Stampe SV-4C N31034 is in its hangar at Carson City, Nevada. It wears French Navy markings.

Produced as a five-seat light transport in 1939, the Cessna T-50 Bobcat was adopted by the US military as a pilot trainer for crews going on to multi-engined aircraft. UC-78 Bobcat N711UU wears Royal Indian Air Force markings at the Mid-America Air Museum, Liberal, Kansas.

The first model to use the Voyager name with the company was the Stinson Model 10A. It launched in February 1941 and was a three-seat cabin monoplane. Pictured wearing RCAF markings, is Stinson 10A Voyager N34690. It is at the Mid-America Air Museum.

One of the most famous and historic aircraft to be preserved is the Ryan NYP NX211. It is better known as the *Spirit of St. Louis* and is the aircraft that Charles Lindbergh flew when making the first solo crossing of the Atlantic Ocean in 1927. It is on display at the National Air and Space Museum, Washington DC site.

Introduced in 1934, the Vultee V-1A was a single-engine, eight-passenger airliner or executive transport aircraft. Picture when on display at the Virginia Aviation Museum, Richmond is V-1AD Special NC16099. It was once owned by the newspaper tycoon Randolph Hearst. When this museum closed, it moved to the Shannon Air Museum, also in Virginia.

The second of three de Havilland twin-engine biplanes, the Dragon Rapide first flew in April 1934. More than 700 had been produced when production ended in 1945. On the move at its Virginia Beach base, and owned by the Military Aviation Museum, is D.H.89 Dragon Rapide NX89DH. It is in the livery of 'G-ADDD', an aircraft owned by the Prince of Wales (later King Edward VIII) in 1935.

One of the most famous training aircraft of all time, the de Havilland Tiger Moth first took to the air in October 1931, and was a development of the D.H.60 Moth. More than 4,000 were built in the UK, with further production in Canada, Australia and New Zealand. Pictured arriving at Oshkosh, is privately owned D.H.82A Tiger Moth NX12731. It wears period Australian markings.

A five-seat cabin monoplane, the Spartan Executive first flew in 1936. The all-metal construction is highlighted by the polish on privately owned Spartan 7.W Executive NC17613, parked at Oshkosh.

Following a proposal in 1955 by Bell, the US Army awarded that company a contract for a utility helicopter. The Bell 205 (UH-1) first flew the following year, and over time the army bought more than 9,000. It was used by all branches of the US military and in countries around the world. Pictured landing after a pleasure flight at Lakeland, Florida is UH-1D Iroquois N624HF. It is owned by the Georgia-based Army Aviation Heritage Foundation.

The Boeing-Vertol Sea Knight was a medium assault transport helicopter for the US Marine Corps. It joined the service at the end of 1964. The aircraft had a powered blade-folding system to the speed up the task of putting the helicopter into the hangars on an aircraft carrier. CH-46A Sea Knight 150941 is at the Havelock Tourist & Event Centre, North Carolina. It wears the high visibility markings of a rescue machine. Note the devise attached to the hoist.

Entering US Navy service in 1963, the Kaman Seasprite had a number of roles including serving on frigates and destroyers as an anti-submarine helicopter. Pictured at Ely Memorial Park, Norfolk NAS, Virginia, is SF-2H Seasprite 149026.

First flown in May 1962, the Sikorsky Skycrane was a heavy-lift helicopter that could carry interchangeable pods to make loading and unloading a very rapid operation. Without the pod, it could carry underslung loads. Following an evaluation of six aircraft by the US Army, production started with an order for 54 to be named Tarhe. More orders followed. On display with the Museum of the Kansas National Guard at Topeka, is CH-54A Tarhe 68-18439.

Above: Used by the USAF as a dedicated crash rescue and firefighting helicopter, the Kaman Huskie had a very distinctive intermeshing rotor system. Operated by the Olympic Flight Museum, Olympia, Washington, is HH-43F Huskie N4069R still in its USAF markings.

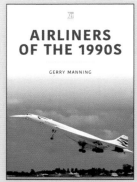
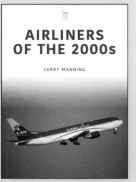
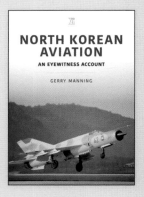